A Kingdom Guide to Stewarding
Your Finances God's Way

Stop Begging God for Money

A Kingdom Guide to Stewarding
Your Finances God's Way

Stop Begging God for Money

Dr. Lexi Johnson

Copyright © 2025 Dr. Lexi Johnson All rights reserved.

No part of this book may be reproduced, distributed or transmitted in any form by any means, graphic, electronic, or mechanical, including photocopy, recording, taping, or by any information storage or retrieval system, without permission in writing from the author except in the case of reprints in the context of reviews, quotes, or references.

While the author has made every effort to ensure that the ideas, statistics, and information presented in this Book are accurate to the best of his/her abilities, any implications direct, derived, or perceived, should only be used at the reader's discretion. The author cannot be held responsible for any personal or commercial damage arising from communication, application, or misinterpretation of the information presented herein.

TITLE: Stop Begging God For Money

First Printed: 2025

Editor: Leslie Cottrell

ISBN: 979-8-9927417-0-4

ISBN eBook: 979-8-9927417-1-1

A Zephaniah Publishing Imprint
Printed in the United States of America

Dedication

I dedicate this book to the women entrepreneurs I have the honor of serving—those who dare to break free from financial bondage and embrace radical stewardship.

To the women who refuse to conform to the world's and religion's broken financial systems and instead choose to walk in Kingdom principles. May this book be a guiding light on your journey to financial dominion.

To the women who are told they are not enough, who have struggled in silence, who have battled fear, doubt, and scarcity —know that you are called to produce, multiply, and dominate.

I pray you rise in faith, take bold action, and wisely steward what God has placed in your hands. The Kingdom needs you, and the world is waiting.

Acknowledgments

First and foremost, I acknowledge my Creator, Yahuah, the source of all wisdom, provision, and revelation. Without His strength and grace, none of this would be possible.

I wholeheartedly thank my immediate family (spouse and children), parents, and siblings for their unwavering love, support, and encouragement throughout my journey. After the Creator, your belief in me is a constant source of strength.

To my financial mentors, Todd and Sandra Newkirk, whom Yah sent at my most desperate financial moment—thank you for your wisdom, generosity, and willingness to walk with me through one of the most transformative seasons of my life.

I honor every pastor and elder I have had the privilege to serve under throughout my life. Your teachings, leadership, and example have shaped my faith, stewardship, and purpose.

To my close friends who have encouraged me, prayed for me, and stood in the gap for me this season—your faithfulness and intercession have been a lifeline, and I am profoundly grateful.

A special thank you to Elder Joan T. Randall, owner and founder of Victorious You Press, and her anointed team. Your mentorship and guidance on this project have been unmatched. I appreciate your dedication to helping authors like me get their message out.

Table of Contents

Introduction   1

ONE
Transform Your Thinking About Money   5

TWO
Financial Healing and Repentance   13

THREE
Get Organized – Bring Order to Your Finances   21

FOUR
Stewarding Cash Flow   27

FIVE
Budget Within Your Allocations   33

SIX
Producing Income   39

SEVEN
The Multiplication Factor—Your Four Storehouses   45

EIGHT
Estate Planning – Leaving A Kingdom Legacy   53

NINE
Transfer of Wealth—Before and After Death 61

Conclusion
Radical Stewardship and the Call to Action 69

Resources for Radical Godly Stewardship 75

Testimonials from the Financial Rebellion 90-Day Coaching Program 79

Are You Ready to Stop Begging and Start Stewarding? 83

About the Author 85

Introduction

Why I'm Writing This Book

In 2008, I lost everything—job, home, cars, marriage—leaving me with over $300,000 in debt. I had done everything "right"—got a degree, a good job, and paid double tithe, yet I was in financial ruin. For three years, I spiraled into depression, crying myself to sleep, believing my situation was hopeless.

One night, in my most desperate moment, I cried out to Yah, telling Him if this was all my life would be, He might as well take me. But instead, He gave me a simple command: "Get up."

That moment changed everything. I got up, took action, and began learning the principles of Radical Godly Stewardship. Since 2012, I've been a financial coach, helping people break free from financial bondage using biblical and practical strategies. Now, I want to help you do the same.

The Problem With Begging for Financial Breakthroughs

Many believers beg God for financial breakthroughs while mishandling what He's already entrusted to them. They tithe, pray, fast, yet still struggle financially. Why? Because God doesn't reward financial irresponsibility with supernatural increase.

The Bible is clear—prosperity isn't about begging but obedience, diligence, and stewardship. Yahusha's Parable of the Talents (Matthew 25:29 NLT) reveals this truth: "To those who use well what they are given, even more will be given… but from those who do nothing, even what little they have will be taken away."

Financial struggle isn't about a lack of money—it's about a lack of stewardship. Stewardship is the trustworthy management of the resources God has entrusted to us for the sole purpose of expanding His Kingdom. It is not about personal gain, status, or accumulation, but about faithfully using wealth, time, and talents to fulfill God's purposes on earth. True biblical stewardship recognizes that all resources belong to God (Psalm 24:1) and that we are merely caretakers, called to produce, multiply, and dominate (Genesis 1:28) in a way that advances His will.

The Solution

The answer isn't another prayer for a breakthrough—it's radical financial stewardship. When you align your finances with Kingdom principles, you step into your divine mandate:

- Produce.
- Multiply.

- Dominate.

This book will teach you seven radical steps, based on Genesis 1:28, to shift from financial struggle to financial dominion:

1. Transform Your Mindset – Change the way you think about money.
2. Financial Healing and Repentance - Releasing the past, embracing Kingdom stewardship
3. Get Organized – Bring order to your finances.
4. Allocate Wisely – Give every dollar a Kingdom purpose.
5. Budget for Financial Freedom – Set boundaries that empower you.
6. Multiply Your Resources – Implement the biblical storehouse system.
7. Establish a Kingdom Legacy – Secure your wealth for future generations.
8. Transfer Wealth Before & After Death – Impact the Kingdom beyond your lifetime.

Each step includes practical actions, tools, and strategies to help you break free from financial bondage. This book is for informational purposes only. I am not a financial advisor. The information contained in it is not financial advice. You should not consider it to be financial advice. The only way to become my client is through a mutual written agreement. Client testimonials are for informational purposes only. Every client's situation is different. The testimonials are only examples of the types of financial coaching I provide. The results in their testimonies are based on their merits and are not a guarantee of similar results.

All scriptures are taken from the New Living Translation of the Bible.

With that said, no more begging. No more financial slavery. It's time to Produce. Multiply. Dominate according to the covenant made with God, the Father of Abraham, Isaac, Jacob, David, and our Messiah Yahusha.

Let's begin.

ONE

Transform Your Thinking About Money

Most of us have been trained to view money through a worldly lens—to hoard, fear, and idolize it. Then, religion stepped in and told us to reject it altogether. We were taught that money doesn't matter, that desiring it is greedy, and that struggling financially somehow makes us holier.

But what if I told you that both the worldly and religious mindsets are the very thing keeping you in financial bondage?

A Kingdom money mindset is not about playing it safe. It is about breaking chains, flipping tables, and confronting lies as we uncover what it means to adopt a Kingdom mindset about money. The world says money is power, but in the Kingdom, money is a tool for dominion. When you shift your perspective, you align yourself with Romans 12:2—being transformed by renewing your mind so you can walk boldly in financial dominion.

Confronting the Lies

You can no longer afford to perpetuate the lies. These lies are the reason you pray for financial breakthroughs but never see them.

Let's expose them one by one.

Lie #1: Money is the root of all evil.

If you've heard this all your life, it's no wonder you're in constant conflict regarding money. You don't want to be "evil," so you suppress your financial desires.

- You refuse to advocate for a raise at work.
- You under charge in your business, giving away everything for next to nothing.
- You judge wealthy people, assuming they are corrupt, while secretly wishing you had their financial success.
- You struggle to give because you barely have enough for yourself.

Meanwhile, the Kingdom is advancing without your financial participation because you've convinced yourself that having money is ungodly.

Here's the truth: The Bible never said money is evil.

The Bible says in 1 Timothy 6:10, "For the love of money is the root of all evil."

Money isn't the problem-idolatry is. Money is a neutral tool—just like fire. Fire in a fireplace brings warmth, but fire in a house burns it down. How it's used makes a difference.

Kingdom Truth: "Money is a defense when coupled with wisdom" (Ecclesiastes 7:11-12). If the enemy keeps you broke, he keeps you defenseless.

Lie #2: There isn't enough to go around.

Scarcity is a demonic deception designed to keep you in financial survival mode.

If you believe resources are limited, you will:

- Compete instead of collaborate because you think someone else's win is your loss.
- Hoard instead of investing because you fear you'll never have enough.
- Operate in greed because you don't trust that God will continue to provide.

But let's be honest—doesn't the world preach scarcity while simultaneously encouraging consumerism? They tell you there's not enough money but ask you to go into debt for luxury items you don't need. That's how they keep you enslaved.

Kingdom Truth: God is abundant, and His resources never run out. The cattle on a thousand hills belong to Him (Psalm 50:10). Kingdom Citizens should not live in financial struggle.

Lie #3: You are holier when you're struggling.

If being broke was holy, then why does God call Himself Jehovah Jireh, our Provider? Jehovah Jireh means he foresaw what you needed and made provision for it. If financial struggles were part of His plan, then Deuteronomy 8:18 would not make sense. In Deut. 8:18, God says, "Remember the LORD your God. He is the one who gives you power to be successful in order to fulfill the covenant he confirmed to your ancestors with an oath." In the King James translation, it says, "power to get wealth." Wealth is any resource including money.

This religious deception that struggling is holier keeps entire churches impoverished while Kingdom work remains underfunded.

- Missions go unsupported.
- Church buildings go into foreclosure.
- Generations inherit debt instead of wealth.

But the Bible does not equate struggle with holiness.

Kingdom Truth: Money is a tool to produce, multiply, and dominate (Genesis 1:28). If God didn't want you to have it, He wouldn't have given you the ability to create it.

The Mindset Shift: Money as a Tool for Dominion

Money is not just about paying bills and surviving. It is a weapon for building kingdoms. When placed in the hands of a wise steward, it funds missions, feeds people experiencing poverty, advances Kingdom businesses, and leaves a legacy for generations.

Look at Yahusha—even He had financial backing. Wealthy supporters funded His ministry (Luke 8:3). If the Son of God needed resources, why do you think you don't?

Accumulating resources, in this case, is not about a prosperity gospel. It is about Kingdom economics.

- In the world, money is used for status.
- In the Kingdom, money is used for strategy.

When you renew your mind, you stop operating in fear, scarcity, and consumerism and start operating in abundance, generosity, security, and dominion.

Practical Challenge: Renewing Your Money Mindset

How do you transform your thinking about money?

Use the Identify, Replace, Renew framework.

Step 1: Identify the Lies

Write down the financial beliefs you grew up hearing. Be honest. Here are some examples.

- "Money is hard to get."
- "I'll always be in debt."
- "Wanting money is selfish."
- "Wealthy people are greedy."

Step 2: Replace with Kingdom Truth

Search the Bible and replace those lies with God's financial truth.

Example:

- *Lie:* "You can do what you like with your money because it's yours."
- *Truth:* Everything belongs to God (Deut. 10:14, Job 41:11, Hebrews 2:10).

Step 3: Renew Your Mind

Commit to a new Kingdom financial confession based on Matthew 6:33:

"I seek the Kingdom of God first and His righteousness, and all these things will be added to me."

Confess it daily. Act in faith. Expect God to fulfill His Word.

Breaking Free from Financial Bondage

When you renew your mind, you stop making fear-based financial decisions. You stop:

- Underpricing your work.

- Feeling guilty for desiring wealth.
- Dismissing financial wisdom as "too worldly."
- Seeing money as evil instead of a tool.

Instead, you:

- Walk in confidence, knowing provision is yours.
- Give generously, without fear of lack.
- Build wealth with wisdom and purpose.
- Produce, Multiply, and Dominate.

Here are a couple of examples of activities you can do to assist you in renewing your mind:

- Commit to a 30-day mindset transformation challenge
- Partner with an accountability group or mentor

It's time to stop begging God for money and steward what you have wisely. Shifting your mindset is the foundation for breaking free from financial bondage.

Let's move forward.

TWO

Financial Healing and Repentance

Before entering financial dominion, you must heal from personal and generational financial wounds. Many have experienced financial trauma through poverty, debt, poor financial decisions, or generational patterns of financial struggle. However, managing money in a Kingdom way is impossible while still carrying financial wounds from a broken system. Healing and repentance are crucial.

Financial repentance is not just about apologizing for past mistakes. It requires deliberately turning away from financial habits, mindsets, and agreements contradicting Kingdom principles. True repentance involves six key actions:

1. Acknowledging and confessing your wounds and mistakes
2. Turning away from your mistakes
3. Releasing financial trauma and curses
4. Renouncing covenants or contracts made with the enemy

5. Declaring your alignment with Kingdom financial principles
6. Affirming your new financial identity

Each of these steps is essential to experiencing true financial freedom.

Acknowledging and confessing your financial wounds and mistakes

The first step toward healing is acknowledging and confessing your financial wounds and mistakes. This step is crucial because it shows you accept responsibility and can now engage in the process of receiving grace and cleansing. These wounds and errors can stem from the following:

- Growing up in scarcity and developing a lack mindset
- Believing that money is evil or that desiring financial success is sinful
- Overspending or mismanaging money due to stress or emotional wounds
- Making financial decisions out of fear, greed, or insecurity
- Generational cycles of debt, poverty, or financial hardship
- Engaging in unethical or dishonest financial practices

Many people operate under financial bondage simply because they lack knowledge of the Kingdom's economic principles. You cannot repent from what you do not recognize as wrong.

Scripture Reflection:

"My people are destroyed for lack of knowledge" (Hosea 4:6).

Practical Step: Write down your financial struggles, identify patterns that need healing, and tell God about it.

Repenting – Turning Away from Worldly and Religious Financial Thinking

Repentance means changing your mind and avoiding financial habits that do not align with Kingdom principles. It is not just about regretting financial mistakes but also about making a deliberate decision to shift from a worldly and religious financial mindset to a Kingdom mindset.

Common Areas of Financial Repentance:

- Overspending and living beyond your means
- Operating in greed, hoarding, or fear-driven financial behaviors
- Neglecting stewardship and failing to manage money wisely
- Trusting in money more than in Yahusha as your provider
- Withholding generosity due to fear of lack

Scripture Reflection:

"Repent, then, and turn to God, so that your sins may be wiped out, that times of refreshing may come from the Lord" (Acts 3:19).

Financial repentance leads to refreshing—new opportunities, wisdom, and a fresh monetary start.

Practical Step: Pray a repentance prayer, expressly renouncing financial sins and asking Yah for a renewed mind. A simple financial repentance prayer is included in the resources section.

Releasing Financial Trauma and Curses

Many people carry generational financial trauma. Perhaps your family struggled financially for years, and you inherited that mindset of lack. Maybe you were taught that being broke was a sign of holiness. These financial burdens are not your inheritance in the Kingdom.

It is time to release:

- The shame of past financial mistakes
- The fear of money and success
- The generational patterns of financial struggle
- The belief that money is evil or unimportant

Scripture Reflection:

"Whom the Son sets free is free indeed" (John 8:36).

Financial deliverance requires letting go of every financial lie, curse, or trauma spoken over you by others and yourself. You may need to forgive those who mismanaged money in your life and caused you financial hardship. You may also need to forgive yourself for mismanaging money throughout your life.

Practical Step: Write down financial lies, curses, or traumas that have affected you. Speak out loud that you release them in Yahusha's name.

Renouncing Any Covenants or Contracts with the Enemy

Many unknowingly enter into financial agreements that bind them to a system of lack and debt. These agreements could include:

- Declaring over your life that you will "always be broke."
- Making money your source instead of God
- Engaging in unethical financial practices
- Operating in debt with no plan for financial freedom
- Accepting financial limitations spoken over your life

Scripture Reflection:

"Death and life are in the power of the tongue" (Proverbs 18:21).

You must verbally renounce any spoken words, agreements, or financial contracts not in alignment with the Kingdom.

Practical Step: Speak a financial renunciation prayer, breaking agreements with poverty, lack, or financial bondage.

Realigning with Kingdom Financial Principles

Repentance and renunciation create a clean slate. It is time to realign your financial habits and mindset with the Kingdom.

Kingdom Financial Realignment Includes:

- Giving: Honoring God with the first fruits of your income (Proverbs 3:9-10) and giving to the poor (Mark 10:21)
- Wise Stewardship: Managing finances responsibly (Luke 16:10)
- Wealth Building: Investing, saving, and creating multiple income streams (Ecclesiastes 11:2)
- Debt Freedom: Avoiding unnecessary debt and living within your means (Proverbs 22:7)

Scripture Reflection:

"Seek first the Kingdom of God and His righteousness, and all these things shall be added unto you" (Matthew 6:33).

When you align your financial decisions with Kingdom principles, you invite supernatural provision, wisdom, and opportunities.

Practical Step: Choose one financial habit you will change this week to align with Kingdom principles.

Affirming Your New Financial Identity

One of the most powerful tools for financial healing is declaring the Kingdom truth over your finances. The enemy will remind you of your mistakes, but you must affirm what God says about your financial future.

Scripture Reflection:

"Let the redeemed of the Lord say so" (Psalm 107:2).

Affirmations (Based on Scripture):

- I am a wise steward of the resources God has given me (Luke 16:10).
- I am free from the spirit of debt and financial lack (Romans 13:8).
- God is my provider; I lack nothing (Philippians 4:19).
- Wealth and riches are in my house because I fear the Lord (Psalms 112:3).

Practical Step: Create a list of personalized financial affirmations using Scripture and declare them daily.

Final Call to Action: Walk in Financial Freedom

Healing and repentance are not one-time events—they are daily decisions to live according to the Kingdom's financial principles.

- Recognize financial wounds and mindsets that need healing
- Repent and turn away from worldly financial thinking

- Release financial trauma, shame, and generational curses
- Renounce agreements with lack, fear, and financial bondage
- Realign with Kingdom financial principles
- Affirm Kingdom financial truth over your life

You cannot produce, multiply, and dominate if you are in financial bondage. God desires you to be healed, whole, and financially free to be a resource for the Kingdom.

Scripture Reflection:

"Beloved, I wish above all things that you may prosper and be healthy, even as your soul prospers" (3 John 1:2).

Practical Challenge:

Take time this week to complete the Financial Healing and Repentance Exercise:

- Write down financial wounds, mistakes, or patterns in your life. Confess them to God.
- Pray a financial repentance prayer.
- Forgive others and yourself for mismanaging money in a way that caused hardship.
- Verbally renounce spoken or written financial agreements that do not align with the Kingdom.
- Create financial affirmations based on Scripture.

This is your new beginning. Now, let's build on this.

THREE

Get Organized – Bring Order to Your Finances

Why Your Finances Aren't Organized

Getting organized financially is one of the most crucial steps in becoming a Radical Godly Steward. Yet, it's also one of the most avoided. Why? Because it forces you to confront the reality of your financial situation and take full responsibility for it. Many people struggle with financial organization for three primary reasons:

1. Facing Your Finances Is Uncomfortable

Looking at your finances means confronting your choices and actions and admitting that you are the problem. That's a hard pill to swallow. It's easier to blame your upbringing, the economy, low-paying jobs, and lack of financial education. But the truth is, no matter what external factors influenced you, you are still responsible for what you do with your money now. Avoiding your financial reality prolongs the cycle of disorder and financial struggle.

2. Awareness Alone Won't Fix It

Even if you've accepted that your financial situation is in your hands, you may still procrastinate when it comes to getting organized. Why? Because change is hard. Deep down, you may be hoping that just being aware of the problem will cause things to change. But faith without works is dead (James 2:26). Your finances won't organize themselves—you must take intentional action.

3. Disorganization Creates More Disorganization

When you live in financial disorder, correcting is even more challenging. Think of your finances like a cluttered room. If every time you take something out, you never put it back where it belongs, your space will eventually become a chaotic mess. The same thing happens with money. If you have bills in different places, accounts you're unsure about, and no transparent system for tracking income and expenses, it can feel overwhelming even to start organizing it. But avoiding the mess makes it worse.

Scripture clarifies that God is a God of order, not confusion (1 Corinthians 14:33). That means financial chaos does not align with His will for your life. Stewardship requires structure, discipline, and accountability. Without organization, you cannot manage what God has entrusted you. The enemy thrives in disorder because confusion leads to destruction. But when you bring order to your finances, you walk in financial freedom and Kingdom abundance.

Steps to Get Organized

1. Gather Everything in One Place

Before creating order, you need to see what you're working with. Creating order means gathering your financial documents, bank statements, bills, pay stubs, tax records, insurance policies, loan agreements, and any other financial paperwork in one place. Create a physical folder and a digital system to access these documents easily. If you don't know where things are, you can't properly manage them.

2. Track Every Dollar

You can't manage what you don't measure. Make a list of all your sources of income and every single expense. Include fixed expenses (rent, car payments, insurance) and variable expenses (groceries, entertainment, giving). Don't just estimate—track it down to the dollar. Most people are shocked when they see where their money is going.

3. Establish Financial Goals

Disorganization is often a result of not having clear financial goals. Ask yourself:

- What are my short-term financial goals (next 6-12 months)?
- What are my long-term financial goals (5-10 years)?
- How does my financial plan align with my Kingdom purpose?

Write these goals down, pray over them, and revisit them regularly to ensure you're staying on track.

4. Create an allocation system that honors God

Allocating isn't about restriction—it's about stewardship. When you create a set of allocations, you tell your money where to go instead of wondering where it went. We will discuss this more in step 4 of this book. Align your budget with Kingdom principles:

- Give freely
- Cover your necessities (food, shelter, transportation).
- Plan for savings and investments.
- Leave an inheritance

5. Set Up Systems for Financial Management

Once you have clarity, set up systems to keep your finances in order:

- Automate Your Payables: Avoid late fees by setting up auto-pay for recurring bills.
- Use Financial Apps or Spreadsheets: Track spending, savings, and investment goals in real time.
- Schedule Weekly Check-ins: Review your finances weekly so you stay on track.
- Organize Your Bank Accounts: Have designated accounts for giving, needs, savings and investments, and wants. Step 3 will discuss this more in-depth.

6. Eliminate Unnecessary Spending

Disorganization often leads to waste. Audit your subscriptions, impulse spending, and any expenses that don't align with your financial goals. Stewardship requires intentional spending. Every dollar you waste is a dollar that you could use for God's purpose in your life.

7. Create an Emergency Fund

Unexpected expenses should not send you into a financial crisis. Set aside at least $1000 - $2,000 initially, then work toward saving 3-6 months' worth of living expenses and ultimately 12 months' worth. An emergency fund prevents you from using credit cards or taking out loans when emergencies arise.

8. Address and Organize Your Debt

Debt is a form of financial bondage. While some debt (such as strategic investments) can serve a purpose, uncontrolled consumer debt hinders financial growth. List out all your debts, including interest rates and minimum payments. Develop a debt elimination plan using the debt snowball or avalanche method. Financial freedom begins with a clear strategy for breaking free from debt.

Scripture should be the foundation of your financial organization. Here are affirmations based on God's Word:

- I am a wise and faithful steward. I manage my finances with diligence and order. (Luke 16:10)

- God is not the author of confusion but of peace. I walk in financial clarity and wisdom. (1 Corinthians 14:33)
- I honor Yahusha with my finances, and He directs my steps in financial stewardship. (Proverbs 3:9-10)
- I am disciplined and self-controlled in all areas of my finances. (2 Timothy 1:7)

Getting organized is not just a suggestion—it's a requirement for a financial breakthrough. Your financial future will be in chaos if your money is in turmoil. Stewardship begins with structure. Today, take the first step:

- Gather all your financial documents.
- Track every dollar for the next 30 days.
- Identify areas of financial waste.
- Set up systems to maintain order.
- Declare and pray over your finances daily.

Radical Godly Stewardship is not about asking God for more money—it's about managing what He has already placed in your hands well. Bring order to your finances, and you will position yourself for Kingdom abundance and financial dominion.

Are you ready to get organized and steward your finances God's way? Take action now, and then let's move to Step 4.

FOUR

Stewarding Cash Flow

One of the most common reasons people struggle financially is a lack of intentionality with their money. Without a clear purpose for every dollar and cent that comes in, your income will slip through your fingers before you even realize it. It will disappear as if into thin air, leaving behind nothing but stress, unpaid bills, and the hamster wheel of waiting for the next paycheck, only to watch it vanish just as quickly.

As a Kingdom Citizen, you cannot afford to live like this. Scarcity and lack are not principles of the Kingdom of God. Your cash must flow with purpose. If you do not take control, your money will control you. To accomplish this, you must implement a system of allocation. An allocation system is essentially the age-old envelope system—but on steroids.

What is Allocation?

Allocation is a proactive strategy for managing your finances. It is a system in which you tell your money exactly where to go rather than allowing it to dictate your financial reality. Financial mismanagement is inevitable without allocation, leading to waste, disorder, and even unnecessary debt.

The key to effective allocation is establishing a percentage-based framework. This approach ensures that every dollar has a designated purpose, regardless of your income level, which is especially critical for business owners and those with fluctuating incomes. We are reminded in, Proverbs 21:5, "Good planning and hard work lead to prosperity, but hasty shortcuts lead to poverty."

The Kingdom Allocation Framework

The Kingdom Allocation Framework consists of four major categories:

1. Household Expenses (Needs)
2. Giving (ministry, charity, birthdays, weddings)
3. Saving and Investing (emergency fund and other savings, retirement and other investments)
4. Discretionary Spending (Wants)

Below is a recommended percentage-based allocation plan:

While these percentages provide a solid foundation, you should adjust them based on your financial situation and long-term goals. Suppose your current spending patterns are way outside these allocations. In that case, you have three options: produce more income, cut expenses, or combine both. Luke states in Luke 14:28, "But don't begin until you count the cost. For who would begin building construction without first calculating the cost to see if there is enough money to finish it?"

Category	Purpose	Suggested Allocation (%)
Household Expenses	Covers essential living costs such as mortgage/rent, utilities, insurance, groceries, and tuition.	60%
Giving	Includes church offerings, charitable donations, and personal giving for birthdays, weddings, etc.	15%
Saving & Investing	Builds financial security through emergency funds, investments, and life insurance strategies.	15%
Discretionary (Wants)	Covers non-essentials such as entertainment, dining out, travel, and subscriptions.	10%

The ultimate objective is to reduce household expenses over time, increase passive income streams through strategic investing, give more, and multiply more. Your passive income should generate enough to cover many of your obligations and discretionary spending without relying solely on active earnings. Proverbs 13:22, reinforces this principle: "Good people leave an inheritance to their grandchildren, but the sinner's wealth passes to the godly."

Why Use the Kingdom Allocation Framework?

Implementing this framework provides several key benefits:

- **Establishes Financial Priorities:** It ensures that your spending aligns with your goals and values rather than being dictated by impulse or circumstance.
- **Eliminates Wasteful Spending:** A structured plan helps curb unnecessary expenses and builds discipline in financial decision-making.
- **Brings Financial Clarity:** You will always know exactly where your money is going, eliminating uncertainty and financial chaos.
- **Ensures Every Need is Met:** This approach honors God's instruction to provide for your family, give generously, meet obligations, and build wealth for future generations.
- **Allows for Regular Review and Adjustment:** Financial circumstances change over time, and you can adapt this framework accordingly. A quarterly review of your allocations will ensure you remain on track with your goals.

The Spiritual Component of Allocation

Finances are not merely a numbers game but a matter of stewardship. Before setting your allocation percentages, pray and seek God's wisdom. Ask for discernment in determining how to distribute your income in a way that honors Him. We are reminded in 2 Corinthians 9:7, "You must each decide in your heart how much to give. And don't give reluctantly or in response to pressure. 'For God loves a person who gives cheerfully.'"

Establish your allocation plan and commit it to God in prayer, trusting that He will bless your efforts and provide the increase. The Bible states in Prov. 16:9, "We can make our plans, but the Lord determines our steps."

It is also crucial to recognize that allocation is an act of faith. By structuring your finances according to Kingdom principles, you acknowledge that God is your ultimate provider. This trust allows you to allocate funds towards giving, even when it may seem financially inconvenient. It enables you to save and invest for the future rather than operate in fear and scarcity. Stewardship requires faith, discipline, and obedience.

Taking Action: How to Implement the Kingdom Allocation Framework

1. **Pray Over Your Plan** – Seek divine wisdom in structuring your finances. Invite God into your financial decisions and commit to following His guidance.
2. **Create Your Allocation Plan**—Determine the percentages that best suit your financial situation. Start with the recommended structure and adjust as necessary.

3. **Implement Your Allocations** – Begin directing your money according to the framework. Set up automated transfers for savings and investments, and use budgeting apps or tools to track your spending.
4. **Review Quarterly**—Adjust allocations as income or expenses change. Stewardship growth is an ongoing process, and regular evaluation ensures alignment with goals.
5. **Remain Faithful** – Trust the process, even when it seems challenging. Kingdom principles work, but they require consistency and obedience.

Final Thoughts

By applying the Kingdom Allocation Framework, you will take control of your cash flow and ensure that every dollar serves a purpose. Financial freedom is not a matter of luck but the result of intentional stewardship. As you faithfully steward your resources, you will position yourself for increase, abundance, and Kingdom impact.

This framework is not just about managing money; it is about aligning your financial decisions with God's principles so that you can produce, multiply, and dominate in your financial life.

Have you set your allocations? If not, take action now. Then, let's move to the next step.

FIVE

Budget Within Your Allocations

One of the biggest financial mistakes people make is spending without a plan. Many earn a decent income, yet they find themselves short on cash month after month, wondering where it all went. The key to breaking this cycle is budgeting within your allocations—ensuring that every dollar you earn has a specific purpose and is aligned with the financial framework you established in Step 4.

Why Budgeting Within Your Allocations Matters

Budgeting is not about restriction but freedom from financial stress, impulsivity, and lack of control. A budget clarifies, prevents waste, and helps you discipline spending to prioritize what truly matters. In Proverbs 27:23 the Bible says, "Know the state of your flocks, and put your heart into caring for your herds." Just as a shepherd must diligently manage his flock, you must intentionally manage your financial resources.

To illustrate how budgeting within allocations works, let's follow Michelle, a 45-year-old entrepreneur living in the

Midwest. She is divorced and has three children, two of whom are grown up and out of the house. Her youngest, age 17, still lives with her. Michelle earns $69,000 annually ($5,750 per month) and has $61,000 in debt, including credit cards and personal loans. Her mortgage payment is $2,200 per month.

Michelle's Budget Using the Kingdom Allocation Framework

Based on Step 4's recommended allocation percentages:

Category	Allocation %	Allocated Amount ($)
Household Expenses	60%	$3,450
Giving	15%	$862.50
Saving & Investing	15%	$862.50
Discretionary (Wants)	10%	$575
Total Income	100%	$5,750

Breaking Down Household Expenses ($3,450/month)

Household expenses include necessary living costs and debt repayment. Here is Michelle's breakdown:

Household Expense	Budgeted Amount ($)
Mortgage	$2,200
Utilities (electric, water, gas, phone, internet)	$450
Car Payment & Insurance	$300
Groceries	$300
Minimum Debt Payments	$200
Other Essentials (medical, child expenses)	$150
Total Household Expenses	**$3,450**

Michelle's Giving Plan ($862.50/month)

Michelle believes in Kingdom giving and uses her 15% allocation as follows:

Giving Category	Budgeted Amount ($)
Church Giving	$500
Charity/Community	$200
Personal Giving (birthdays, weddings, etc.)	$162.50
Total Giving	**$862.50**

Michelle's Saving & Investing Plan ($862.50/month)

Savings & Investments	Budgeted Amount ($)
Emergency Fund	$300
Retirement Contributions	$300
Opportunity Investments	$162.50
Life Insurance	$100
Total Savings & Investing	**$862.50**

Michelle's Discretionary Spending ($575/month)

Discretionary Expense	Budgeted Amount ($)
Eating Out	$150
Entertainment	$125
Travel Savings	$100
Self-Care (salon, gym)	$100
Miscellaneous	$100
Total Discretionary	**$575**

Adjusting the Budget to Eliminate Overspending

After filling out the Radical Godly Stewardship (RGS) Personal Budget Worksheet (see the resources section), Michelle realizes that her actual spending exceeds her allocation in two key areas:

1. **Household Expenses:** She has been spending an extra $250 monthly on convenience groceries and takeout. By meal prepping and shopping with a list, she can cut $150 from groceries and $100 from dining out, reallocating that money toward debt repayment.
2. **Discretionary Spending:** Michelle notices that she frequently overspends on personal care and entertainment. She cuts her entertainment budget by $50 and her personal care budget by $50, freeing up $100 for savings.

Using the Budget to Achieve Financial Freedom

By aligning her spending with her allocations, Michelle gains clarity, control, and confidence in her financial future. Budgeting within her allocations helps her:

- **Prioritize Needs Over Wants** – She ensures that essential expenses, giving, and savings come first.
- **Eliminate Wasteful Spending** – Small adjustments prevent unnecessary debt and financial strain.
- **Improve Self-Discipline** – She learns to manage money with intention rather than impulse.

- **Reduce Financial Stress and Guilt** – Knowing where her money goes eliminates anxiety over finances.
- **Accelerate Debt Payoff** – She can make additional debt payments by cutting overspending.

Implementing the Budget: A Step-by-Step Approach

1. Use the RGS Personal Budget Worksheet – Enter your projected income and expenses.
2. Review Actual Spending Each Pay Period – Compare projected vs. actual costs.
3. Make Adjustments – Identify areas of overspending and reallocate funds.
4. Track Progress – Monitor financial improvements every month.
5. Utilize Banking Tools – Many banks allow custom budget categories to track spending in real time.

Biblical Wisdom for Budgeting

- Luke 16:10, "If you are faithful in little things, you will be faithful in large ones." Budgeting within allocations teaches faithfulness in financial stewardship.
- Proverbs 16:3, "Commit your actions to the Lord, and your plans will succeed." Aligning financial decisions with God's principles brings success.
- Ecclesiastes 7:12, "Wisdom and money can get you almost anything, but only wisdom can save your life."

Budgeting is both wise and necessary for financial well-being.

Final Thoughts

A budget is not a restriction—it is a tool that empowers you to take control of your financial future. Sticking to an allocation-based budget creates a stable financial foundation, eliminates waste, and positions you for financial freedom.

Are you ready to budget within your allocations? Download the Radical Godly Stewardship Personal Budget Worksheet and Debt Payoff Tracker, create your plan, and start taking dominion over your finances today!

SIX

Producing Income

A fixed mindset when generating income is one of the most significant obstacles to financial freedom. Many people believe that their financial well-being is entirely dependent on the salary assigned to them by their employer. They see their job as the only source of income, failing to recognize their power to produce wealth beyond their paycheck. While a 9-to-5 job may provide stability, it should not be the only income stream. Every Kingdom citizen should actively seek multiple income streams through a side hustle, investments, or a full-fledged business.

The Biblical Foundation for Producing Multiple Streams of Income

The Bible provides clear guidance on the importance of diversifying income streams. Ecclesiastes 11:2 states, "But divide your investments among many places, for you do not know what risks may lie ahead." This verse highlights the wisdom of having multiple sources of income as a safeguard against financial hardship. Deuteronomy 8:18 further reinforces this principle: "Remember the Lord your God. He is the one who gives you the power to be successful to fulfill the covenant he confirmed to your ancestors with an oath." God has given us the power to create wealth, but it requires action on our part.

The Proverbs 31 woman is a prime example of someone who embraced multiple income streams. Proverbs 31:16-18 states, "She goes to inspect a field and buys it; with her earnings she plants a vineyard. She is energetic and strong, a hard worker. She makes ensures her dealings are profitable; her lamp burns late into the night." She was not limited to a single source of income; instead, she diversified her efforts to ensure financial security for her household.

Types of Income Streams

There are four primary types of income streams that every person should consider incorporating into their financial strategy:

1. **Active income** is the most common type of income earned by exchanging time and labor for money. Examples include salaries, hourly wages, and freelance work.
2. **Passive income** is generated with minimal effort after completing the initial work. Examples include rental income, royalties, investment dividends, and automated online businesses.

3. **Leveraged Income** – Income that grows by utilizing the time, skills, or efforts of others. Examples include network marketing, business ownership with employees, and real estate syndications.
4. **Windfall Income** – Unexpected financial gains such as inheritances, bonuses, lottery winnings, or legal settlements. While unpredictable, proper stewardship of windfall income can lead to long-term financial stability.

The Importance of Aligning Income Streams with Purpose

While multiple streams of income are essential, not every opportunity is beneficial. Income streams should align with one's Kingdom purpose and values. Just because something is profitable does not mean it is the right path. In Proverbs 10:22, it states, "The blessing of the Lord makes a person rich, and he adds no sorrow with it." Seeking income streams aligning with one's purpose ensures financial growth is fulfilling and sustainable.

Overcoming Barriers to Creating Additional Income Streams

Many people desire additional income but face internal and external barriers that prevent them from taking action. The most common barriers include:

- **Fear of Failure** – Many hesitate to start a new venture due to the possibility of failure. However, Proverbs 24:16 reminds us, "The godly man may trip seven times, but they will get up again."
- **Lack of Knowledge**—Some feel they lack the expertise to start a business or invest. You can overcome a lack of knowledge by seeking mentorship, taking courses, and investing time in learning. In Prov. 2:3, the Bible says, "Cry out for insight, and ask for understanding."
- **Time Management** – Balancing a job, family, and additional income streams can feel overwhelming. The key is prioritizing tasks and using efficient systems to manage time effectively. "So be careful how you live. Don't live like fools, but like those who are wise. Make the most of every opportunity in these evil days" (Ephesians 5:15-16)
- **Fear of Overworking** – Some fear that additional income streams will consume their lives. The key is to focus on **income efficiency**—streams that generate revenue with minimal ongoing effort. Work six days, rest on the seventh (Exodus 20:9-10).

Case Study: Michelle's Plan for Producing Income

Michelle, our case study example, has determined that she needs to create an additional income stream to accelerate her financial goals. She earns $69,000 annually but has $61,000 in debt and ongoing financial obligations. She decides to engage in an income stream mapping activity to assess her current financial situation and explore new opportunities. See the resources section for a copy of this activity.

Michelle's Income Stream Mapping Activity:

1. Identify Current Income Streams: Michelle lists her primary salary and any side income she has earned in the past, such as occasional consulting work.
2. Explore Potential New Income Streams: She identifies possible ways to increase her earnings based on her skills and interests. She considers:

- She is starting a small consulting business in her area of expertise.
- Monetizing a skill, such as writing or graphic design, through freelance work.
- Investing in a rental property or a short-term vacation rental.

3. Determine a Realistic Income Goal: Michelle sets a goal to generate an additional $1,000 monthly for debt repayment and investments.
4. Take Actionable Steps:

- She creates a professional profile on a freelance website to offer her services.

- She begins researching real estate investment opportunities that fit within her budget.
- She networks with other entrepreneurs to learn best practices and identify mentorship opportunities.

Final Thoughts: The Power of Producing Income

Producing multiple streams of income is a necessity, not a luxury. Kingdom citizens can break free from financial limitations and walk fully in their God-given authority. Anyone can create financial stability and abundance by taking proactive steps, diversifying income, and overcoming barriers.

As Prov 13:4 states, "Lazy people want much but get little, but those who work hard will prosper." Those who take the initiative to create additional income streams will position themselves for financial breakthroughs and long-term success.

Now, let's take what we have produced and learn how to multiply it.

SEVEN

The Multiplication Factor—Your Four Storehouses

A Commanded Blessing Requires a Storehouse

One of the most overlooked financial principles in the Kingdom is the need for storehouses. In Deuteronomy 28:8, God says, "The Lord will command the blessing upon you in your storehouses and all that you undertake." However, God cannot bless what does not exist. If you do not have storehouses—places where wealth is accumulated and strategically positioned—there is nothing for Him to bless.

In the story of Joseph, the biblical model of storehouses appears in Genesis 41. When Pharaoh had a dream foretelling seven years of abundance followed by seven years of famine, Joseph's divine wisdom led him to establish a system of storehouses. These were filled consistently during plenty, not sporadically or when it was convenient. Because of this strategy, Egypt survived the famine and even prospered. Likewise, in your financial life, you must build your storehouses in times of provision so that when financial droughts come, you are prepared.

The Four Storehouses of Financial Stewardship

To multiply wealth and establish financial security, I recommend four essential storehouses:

1. Emergency Fund
2. Wealth Building/Retirement Fund
3. Opportunity Fund
4. Life Insurance

Each storehouse plays a vital role in financial resilience and Kingdom expansion.

Storehouse #1: Emergency Fund—Your First Line of Defense

A key issue with emergency funds is that those who need them most often do not have them. Saving is not a priority for many; it is an afterthought. Emergencies will happen—it is only a matter of time. Without an emergency fund, people rely on credit cards, loans, or borrowing from others, leading to deeper financial bondage.

What is an emergency? It is not an unplanned vacation or impulse shopping. True emergencies include:

- Unexpected medical expenses
- Major car repairs
- Furnace or major appliance breakdowns
- Urgent home repairs
- Travel expenses for a funeral

Building an Emergency Fund

Your Emergency fund should be saved in a high-yield savings account. You can easily access it while it earns interest. The goal is to have six to twelve months of expenses saved. Let's apply this to Michelle's finances from Step 5:

Months Covered	Required Savings
6 months	$20,700
12 months	$41,400

Michelle has budgeted $300 per month for this storehouse. Here's how long it will take her to reach key milestones, assuming a 3.5% monthly return:

- $1,000 starter emergency fund → 3 months
- 6 months of expenses ($20,700) → 5.5 years
- 12 months of expenses ($41,400) → 11 years

Michelle can accelerate this process by automating savings, increasing contributions when possible, or adding an income stream.

Storehouse #2: Wealth Building & Retirement Fund

The goal of this storehouse is simple: stop working for money and let money start working for you. Wealth-building investments allow you to focus more on Kingdom assignments without financial worry.

Dr. Lexi Johnson

Retirement Planning and Investment Strategies

Society pressures us to retire at 67, but this is not a biblical requirement—with proper planning, financial independence can come much sooner. The retirement amount depends on personal goals, lifestyle, and investment choices. Working with a financial coach or planner can help determine this number.

Michelle wants to retire at age 65 in 20 years. Assuming she needs $50,000 annually in retirement income and expects to live for 25 more years, her goal is $1.25 million in assets.

To reach this, Michelle must consider:

- Time horizon (20 years until retirement)
- Risk tolerance (Conservative, Moderate, Aggressive)
- Investment vehicles (401(k), Roth IRA, stocks, bonds, real estate, etc.)

Types of Investments:

- Paper Assets: Stocks, bonds, mutual funds, ETFs
- Real Estate: Rental properties, REITs
- Alternative Investments: Crypto, art, business startups

The parable of the talents in Matthew 25 is a biblical endorsement of investing. Genesis 1:28 also commands us to multiply, and investing fulfills this mandate through the power of compound interest.

Storehouse #3: Opportunity Fund

An opportunity fund allows you to capitalize on unexpected but advantageous financial opportunities. Many people miss out on life-changing opportunities because they lack available capital.

Let's return to Michelle. Suppose a colleague invites her to invest in purchasing farmland to create jobs and generate income. Michelle is passionate about economic empowerment but cannot participate without an opportunity fund.

She allocates a portion of her savings to an opportunity fund to ensure she can act when a God-ordained opportunity arises.

Storehouse #4: Life Insurance—Protection and Investment

Life insurance can serve two purposes:

1. Protection (Term insurance - no cash value) Life insurance that provides coverage at a fixed rate of payments for a certain period.)
2. Wealth Building (leveraging cash value through tax-free policy loans)

Protecting Your Loved Ones

One of the greatest gifts you can give your family is financial security in your absence. Many families make critical financial decisions while grieving, leading to stress, confusion, and often financial instability. Life insurance ensures your loved ones are not burdened with funeral costs, outstanding debts, or sudden income loss.

Life insurance creates an immediate estate, especially for those who have not yet accumulated wealth. The amount of coverage should be determined using the D.I.M.E. formula, which accounts for:

- Debt and Death Expenses (funeral, medical bills, outstanding loans)
- Income Replacement (years of income needed for dependents)
- Mortgage Payoff (ensuring the family home is secure)
- Education Costs (college tuition for children)

Life Insurance—Wealth Building

An Indexed Universal Life (IUL) policy allows policyholders to borrow against their accumulated cash value, essentially becoming their own bank. This method provides liquidity while maintaining growth potential. However, IULs require consistent contributions of at least $1,000 per month for 10+ years to be effective. IULs are not an investment; they are a savings strategy.

For many, a combination of term life insurance for protection and a Roth IRA or real estate for wealth-building is a more feasible strategy.

The Power of Having Four Storehouses

By establishing these storehouses, you build:

3. Financial Stability & Resilience – Preparedness for emergencies, investments, and future needs
4. Freedom from Financial Stress – No longer living paycheck to paycheck
5. Readiness for Kingdom Assignments – Ability to give, invest, and support ministries without hesitation
6. Intergenerational Wealth – Positioning your children and grandchildren for success

Automating Contributions

To ensure success, automate deposits into each storehouse. Align these investments with overall financial goals and review allocations quarterly.

Final Thoughts

Joseph's storehouses in Egypt ensured survival and positioned him to influence nations. Your financial storehouses will do the same. When managed properly, these four storehouses will give you financial stability, the ability to seize opportunities, and the capacity to fund Kingdom expansion.

Which storehouse do you need to build first? If you do not have any in place, start the life insurance and the emergency fund first. Start your retirement or wealth-building storehouse next.

Start your opportunity fund is last. Take action today and establish your financial foundation for tomorrow!

EIGHT

Estate Planning – Leaving A Kingdom Legacy

The Problem: Why the Lack of Estate Planning is a Crisis

Estate planning is often deemed unimportant or postponed, especially among those who believe it is only necessary for the wealthy. However, failing to have a plan can devastate families, ministries, and businesses. In Proverbs 13:22, the Bible says, "A good man leaves an inheritance to his children's children, but the sinner's wealth is laid up for the righteous." Without estate planning, your assets may not be distributed according to your desires, leading to family disputes, unnecessary taxes, and court battles.

Even high-profile celebrities have fallen victim to the consequences of poor estate planning.

- **Prince** – The legendary musician died in 2016 without a will, leading to a six-year legal battle among his family members. His estate, worth hundreds of millions, was divided after extensive litigation, with

- large portions lost to legal fees and taxes. The risks of dying without making a will. Stewarts. "What are the risks of dying without making a will." March 29, 2022. https://www.stewartslaw.com/news/what-are-the-risks-of-dying-without-making-a-will/.
- **Aretha Franklin**— The Queen of Soul passed, away in 2018. They initially believed she had no will. Handwritten wills were discovered later, leading to confusion and disputes among her heirs. The Eastern New Mexico News. "Soul speaks at ENMU." December 16, 2018. https://www.easternnewmexiconews.com/story/2018/12/16/news/soul-speaks-at-enmu/160214.html.
- **Chadwick Boseman**—The "Black Panther" star passed away in 2020 without a will, which resulted in legal proceedings that delayed the distribution of his assets and caused financial strain on his surviving spouse. NBC News. "What happened to Chadwick Boseman's $2.3 million estate is an exception, not the rule. July 1, 2022. https://www.nbcnews.com/think/opinion/-chadwick-boseman-23-million-estate-exception-not-rule-rcna36196

These examples highlight the chaos that can ensue when estate planning is ignored. Estate planning is about distributing wealth and ensuring that your God-given resources are managed wisely for future generations and Kingdom impact.

Estate Planning is for Everyone

A common misconception is that estate planning is only for those with substantial wealth. This misconception is far from the truth. Even if you do not own a home or have significant assets, estate planning ensures that your health, finances, and legacy wishes are honored. It is about stewardship—managing what God has entrusted to you. Whether you have a modest estate or vast resources, the principles remain the same: prepare for the future so that what you have built is preserved and used according to the purpose of the Kingdom.

Let's walk through the essential estate planning steps using Michelle, our case study from previous chapters. Michelle is a 45-year-old entrepreneur with a teenage child, a mortgage, and growing investments. While she is still working toward financial independence, estate planning is crucial to protect her assets, secure her child's future, and ensure her Kingdom values continue beyond her lifetime.

Step 1: Creating or Updating a Will

What is a Will?

A will is a legally binding document that outlines how to distribute your assets after your death. It allows you to:

- Designate beneficiaries (who will inherit your assets)
- Appoint an executor (who will carry out your wishes)
- Name a guardian for minor children

- Specify any charitable or ministry contributions

Why is a Will Important?

Without a will, state laws (intestate succession) determine how your assets are divided. This can lead to unintended consequences, such as estranged relatives inheriting your property or assets tied up in legal battles. A will provide clarity and prevent unnecessary stress for your loved ones. It also allows you to ensure that your wealth is directed toward causes that align with your Kingdom values rather than being squandered or lost in probate fees.

Cost of a Will

- Attorney-prepared will: $300–$1,000, depending on complexity
- Online legal services (LegalShield, LegalZoom, Rocket Lawyer): $50–$250
- State-provided free will forms: Some states provide simple templates at no cost

Michelle's Action Plan: She uses an attorney to create a will, ensuring that her business, home, and financial accounts are distributed according to her wishes. She also names a guardian for her 17-year-old child.

Step 2: Establishing a Trust

What is a Trust?

A trust is a legal entity that holds assets on behalf of beneficiaries. It provides greater control over how and when assets are distributed, offering protection from probate and ensuring privacy. Unlike a will, a trust can also provide benefits. At the same time, you are still alive, such as asset protection and tax advantages.

Types of Trusts and Their Purposes

- Revocable Living Trust: Allows you to retain control over assets while alive and seamlessly transfer them upon death without probate.
- Irrevocable Trust: Protects assets from creditors and reduces estate taxes.
- Testamentary Trust: Created through a will and activated after death.
- Charitable Trust: Directs assets toward Kingdom purposes, such as ministries or missions.

Cost of Setting Up a Trust

- Basic revocable trust: $1,000–$3,000
- Complex estate trust: $5,000+
- Online options: $500–$1,500

Michelle's Action Plan: Michelle owns a business and sets up a revocable living trust to ensure her child inherits her assets without going through probate. She also allocates a portion of her estate to a charitable trust to continue supporting ministries she cares about.

Step 3: Power of Attorney for Finances & Health

A Power of Attorney (POA) grants a trusted individual the authority to make financial or healthcare decisions if you become incapacitated.

- Financial POA: Handles financial matters such as paying bills, managing investments, and handling property.
- Healthcare POA: Allows a designated person to make medical decisions on your behalf.

Assign these roles to different individuals to prevent conflicts of interest.

Michelle's Action Plan: She names her sister her financial POA and a trusted friend her healthcare POA.

Step 4: Advance Health Directive

An advance health directive (or living will) specifies your medical preferences if you cannot communicate them. It includes:

- Life support decisions
- Do Not Resuscitate (DNR) orders
- Organ donation preferences

Michelle's Action Plan: She completes an advance directive, ensuring her medical preferences align with her faith.

Final Thoughts: The Importance of Estate Planning

Estate planning is not a one-time event but an ongoing process you review annually. Life changes—marriages, births, financial growth, and even shifts in your business—require updates to your estate plan to ensure that it remains aligned with your Kingdom values and goals.

Just as you steward your finances during your lifetime, you must also teach your heirs the principles of Kingdom stewardship. A financial inheritance without wisdom can lead to mismanagement and loss. In Proverbs 22:6, we are reminded, "Train up a child in the way he should go, and when he is old, he will not depart from it." Leaving a legacy is more than transferring assets; it is about passing down wisdom, values, and a Kingdom mindset.

The time to take action is now. Do not let procrastination, fear, or the misconception that estate planning is only for the wealthy prevent you from ensuring your legacy. The resources God has entrusted to you are meant to have a lasting impact beyond your lifetime. Take the steps necessary today to protect your family, secure your assets, and leave a Kingdom legacy that reflects your faith and values.

Moving into Step 8, we will explore Wealth Transfer—positioning the next generation for financial dominion. This final step ties everything together, demonstrating how stewardship, financial planning, and estate management culminate in successfully transferring wealth and wisdom to the next generation.

NINE

Transfer of Wealth—Before and After Death

The Misconception of Wealth Transfer

One of the most misunderstood concepts among believers is the idea of the "transfer of wealth" or "wealth transfer." Many in the church assume that this phrase refers to a miraculous, one-time event in which God will suddenly move wealth from the hands of the wicked into the hands of the righteous. This could not be further from the truth. While Scripture speaks of wealth being laid up for the just (Proverbs 13:22), this transfer is not passive. Wealth transfers occur when Kingdom Citizens are positioned correctly—walking in the right standing with God, operating by Kingdom financial principles, and stewarding wealth responsibly.

Deuteronomy 8:18 declares, "But thou shalt remember the Lord thy God: for it is he that giveth thee power to get wealth, that he may establish his covenant which he sware unto thy fathers, as it is this day." This verse clarifies that wealth is not simply given but acquired through God-given power, wisdom, and responsibility. As believers walk in alignment with Kingdom principles, demonstrating faithfulness in stewardship, God entrusts them with more significant resources. Wealth transfer is not about sudden riches falling into one's lap—it is about preparation, positioning, and executing a plan that ensures the wealth God has entrusted to you serves a Kingdom purpose beyond your lifetime.

Proper wealth transfer is both a process and a responsibility. It involves setting up financial systems that allow what you have built to be transferred to others—before and after death—ensuring that your resources continue to advance the Kingdom of God.

Action Steps for Preparing to Transfer Wealth

Step 1: Identify Individuals, Ministries, or Causes to Invest In

Wealth transfer is about intentional giving. The first step is to identify the individuals, ministries prayerfully and causes that align with Kingdom values. Not every charity or person is worthy of your wealth—this process requires discernment.

Consider the following when choosing where to transfer wealth:

- Does this person or ministry reflect biblical values?
- Are they faithful stewards of what they already have?

- Will your wealth further the Kingdom of God through this investment?
- Does this gift align with your mission and financial goals?

Mentoring and preparing children, grandchildren, or younger family members for financial responsibility is essential for those transferring wealth. Transferring large sums of money to someone who lacks financial wisdom can lead to mismanagement and waste.

Michelle's Example: Michelle has a 17-year-old child for whom she is preparing to take on financial responsibility. She teaches budgeting, the importance of tithing, and how to manage income wisely. She has also opened an investment account in her child's name and regularly walks through financial decisions together to instill wisdom before transferring wealth.

Another way to prepare younger generations is to include them in discussions about investments, real estate, and business dealings. Kingdom wealth is not just about material prosperity but about equipping the next generation to be stewards of the resources entrusted to them. When children and grandchildren understand financial principles early, they are better equipped to handle wealth responsibly and use it for Kingdom purposes.

Step 2: Plan Strategic Gifts That Align with Purpose

Once you have identified the right recipients, the next step is to plan your giving strategically. Strategically giving means deciding what you will provide and how you will give it. There are several vehicles for transferring wealth effectively:

- Donor-advised funds (DAFs) allow you to contribute assets, receive immediate tax benefits, and distribute funds to charities over time.
- Charitable Gift Annuities: These provide donors with a fixed income for life while donating the remainder to a chosen charity.
- Charitable Remainder Trusts (CRTs): These allow assets to be placed in trust, providing income to beneficiaries for a specified period before the remainder goes to a charity.
- Qualified Charitable Distributions (QCDs): If you are over 70 ½ years old, you can donate funds directly from your retirement account to a qualified charity, reducing taxable income.

Giving while you are alive allows you to witness the impact of your generosity. It ensures that your wealth is stewarded effectively, rather than waiting for others to distribute it after your passing. The joy of seeing your resources bless others in your lifetime is priceless.

Step 3: Model God's Example—Plan Ahead

We serve a God who plans. He is not reactive; He is a God of pro-vision—meaning He provides before the need arises. His provision is evident throughout Scripture, from Joseph storing grain in Egypt (Genesis 41) to Yahusha preparing His disciples for what was to come (John 14:1-3).

Planning for wealth transfer ensures that the passing down of your resources is not an afterthought. It allows for financial peace of mind, prevents disputes, and ensures that wealth continues to fund Kingdom work long after you are gone.

Michelle's Example: Michelle has decided to create a charitable remainder trust, allowing her to provide for her child while ensuring that a percentage of her wealth funds Kingdom projects upon her passing. She has also documented her wishes clearly to prevent confusion or disputes.

Another proactive approach is business succession planning. If you own a business, consider how it will be passed down or sold. Too often, companies fail after the founder's passing because there is no succession plan. Kingdom entrepreneurs must think generationally, ensuring businesses continue functioning effectively under new leadership.

Using Resources and Professional Guidance

Wealth transfer is not a DIY project. It requires wisdom and expertise. Consider using wealth transfer planning tools such as:

- A Wealth Transfer Plan Template (to be provided in the resource section of this book)
- Professional estate planners or financial advisors
- Succession planning guides for business owners

Seeking guidance from Kingdom-minded financial professionals ensures that your estate plan aligns with biblical stewardship principles and protects against common pitfalls such as unnecessary taxation, probate delays, and family disputes.

Some families create financial mission statements outlining their collective wealth stewardship vision. These statements serve as a guiding principle for future generations and help ensure financial decisions align with biblical values.

The Benefits of Preparing for Wealth Transfer Before and After Death

1. You fulfill your role as a Kingdom builder
2. Your wealth continues to advance God's Kingdom long after you are gone.
3. You experience the joy of blessing others while alive
4. Giving is not just about what happens after death. You get to witness the fruit of your generosity.
5. You leave an inheritance for your children's children (Proverbs 13:22)
6. Generational wealth ensures that your descendants are positioned for financial stability and Kingdom impact.
7. You maintain control over how your wealth is used

8. Without a plan, your wealth may be unnecessarily misused, squandered, or taxed.
9. You ensure all giving is aligned and strategic
10. A well-planned transfer ensures your resources go where they will have the most impact.

Final Thoughts: Stewarding the Transfer of Wealth

Wealth transfer is not a singular event but a lifetime commitment to wise resource stewardship. The Kingdom of God requires faithful, prepared, and strategic stewards. Whether you are passing wealth to your children, ministries, or charitable causes, your planning and wisdom will determine whether your financial legacy advances God's work or is wasted.

The time to start is now. Take action to position yourself for effective, intentional wealth transfer—both before and after death—so that your impact on the Kingdom of God continues for generations.

Conclusion

Radical Stewardship and the Call to Action

Summarizing the Nine Steps to Financial Dominion

This book has uncovered the nine steps to radical Godly stewardship. These steps are not theoretical concepts but practical, actionable principles designed to position you as a faithful steward of the wealth God entrusts to you. They are not merely about achieving personal financial success but fulfilling your Kingdom mandate to produce, multiply, and dominate.

1. **Transform Your Thinking About Money**
    - Money is not evil; the love of money is.
    - Your mindset shapes your financial reality.
    - Replace worldly money beliefs with Kingdom truths.
2. **Financial Healing and Repentance**
    - Confront financial trauma and past mistakes.
    - Repent for mismanagement and commit to new habits.

- Release limiting beliefs and align with Kingdom stewardship.

3. **Get Organized—Bring Order to Your Finances**
    - Avoid the chaos of disorganization.
    - Gain clarity by tracking every dollar.
    - Develop financial order to set the foundation for success.

4. **Stewarding Cash Flow—Allocating With Purpose**
    - Give every dollar a mission.
    - Implement the Kingdom Allocation Framework.
    - Shift from scarcity to financial dominion.

5. **Budget Within Your Allocations**
    - A budget is a tool for freedom, not restriction.
    - Monitor spending and adjust where necessary.
    - Use budgeting tools and systems to stay on track.

6. **Producing Income**
    - Producing multiple income streams is a necessity.
    - Be proactive in diversifying your income.
    - It's a precursor for financial stability and abundance.

7. **The Multiplication Factor—Your Four Storehouses**
    - Establish financial stability and resilience.
    - Build emergency funds, investment portfolios, and opportunity funds.

- Multiply wealth through wise stewardship.

8. **Estate Planning—Leaving a Kingdom Legacy**
    - Avoid probate and unnecessary legal battles.
    - Use wills, trusts, and succession planning to protect assets.
    - Ensure your financial legacy aligns with Kingdom purposes.

9. **Transfer of Wealth—Before and After Death**
    - Wealth transfer is not a sudden event; it is a process.
    - Identify beneficiaries and strategic giving opportunities.
    - Steward resources in a way that continues to impact the Kingdom.

Stop Begging, Start Stewarding

Too often, believers beg God for financial breakthroughs while failing to apply the principles He has already given. The problem is not that God has withheld wealth from His people; many have not demonstrated the financial wisdom and discipline necessary to receive and sustain it.

It is time to shift from waiting for miracles to walking in dominion. The world does not need more believers who are financially bound, struggling to make ends meet, and unable to fund Kingdom initiatives. The world needs faithful stewards positioned to produce, multiply, and dominate their finances.

You now have the blueprint. You have been given the keys to unlock financial transformation through radical stewardship. The only thing left to do is act.

Immediate Actions to Take Now

1. Go to the Resources Page
    - Gain access to exclusive financial tools and templates.
    - Download worksheets, budgeting tools, and estate planning guides.
    - Use the Kingdom Allocation Framework to structure your finances.
2. Join the Kingdom Money Masters Patreon Community
    - Engage in ongoing financial coaching.
    - Participate in monthly Q&A sessions and mentorship.
    - Connect with like-minded Kingdom stewards.
3. Enroll in the Financial Rebellion 90-Day Coaching Program.
    - Receive hands-on guidance in implementing these steps.
    - Overcome limiting beliefs and establish financial discipline.
    - Work with experts to ensure long-term financial stability.
4. Commit to a Kingdom Financial Plan

- Review and adjust your financial goals every quarter.
- Implement estate planning measures to secure your legacy.
- Set up your four storehouses and begin allocating wealth strategically.

5. Hold Yourself Accountable
    - Partner with a financial accountability partner or coach.
    - Track your progress in a financial journal.
    - Regularly evaluate where you are on your journey toward financial dominion.

Your Next Steps Determine Your Financial Future

Financial transformation does not happen by accident. It requires intentionality, discipline, and a commitment to applying Kingdom principles. The difference between those who walk in monetary freedom and those who remain bound by financial lack is execution. Will you take action today, or will you continue to let financial disorganization, scarcity, and fear rule your life?

The choice is yours. Stop begging. Start stewarding.

Go to the resources page and take the next step toward financial dominion. Produce, multiply, and dominate. The Kingdom is waiting.

Resources for Radical Godly Stewardship

This resource page provides essential tools, communities, and websites to help you implement the principles of radical stewardship. These resources will equip you to take control of your finances, build wealth, and leave a Kingdom legacy.

Tools and Templates

These downloadable resources will help you wisely organize, allocate, and steward your finances.

- Radical Godly Stewardship Personal Budget Worksheet – Use the Kingdom Allocation Framework to track your income and expenses.
- Debt Payoff Tracker – A strategic tool to help you systematically eliminate debt.
- Kingdom Wealth Transfer Plan Template – Outline your estate planning and wealth transfer strategy.
- Financial Goals Planner – Set short-term and long-term financial goals that align with Kingdom principles.
- Emergency Fund Savings Plan – Calculate how much you need and create a savings schedule.

- Business Succession Planning Guide – A step-by-step roadmap for ensuring a smooth transfer of your business assets

Download these tools now and start stewarding your finances with wisdom and intentionality. https://bit.ly/stopbeggingresources

Online Communities

Connect with like-minded Kingdom stewards committed to financial transformation and radical stewardship.

- Kingdom Money Masters Patreon Community – Access more tools, resources, community support, and expert financial mentorship. patreon.com/KingdomMoneyMasters
- Financial Rebellion 90-Day Coaching Program – A structured program designed to help you master the principles of radical stewardship. https://mm4h.life/financial-coaching
- Kingdom Money Masters Facebook Group – A community for believers committed to aligning their finances with Kingdom principles. https://www.facebook.com/groups/moneymastery4her

Join these communities to stay accountable and receive ongoing support on your financial journey.

Websites

Access additional financial education, tools, and resources from trusted sources.

- **Money Mastery 4 Her Enterprises** – https://www.mm4h.life for coaching, courses, and resources for Kingdom-minded women entrepreneurs
- **Kingdom InPowered Network** – https://www.youtube.com/@KIN-Media for faith-based financial teachings and media content
- **LegalZoom** – https://www.legalzoom.com for online estate planning services, including wills and trusts
- **Ally Bank** - https://www.ally.com/ for personal banking, checking accounts with spending buckets.
- **Profit First** – https://mikemichalowicz.com/profit-first/ – Books and Digital tools for business money management.
- **Relay Bank** - https://bankwith.relayfi.com/ for implementing the Kingdom Allocation System in your business finances
- **High-Yield Savings Accounts Comparison** – https://www.nerdwallet.com/best/banking/high-yield-online-savings-accounts to find the best HYSA options for your emergency fund

Use these websites to deepen your financial knowledge and execute your wealth-building strategy.

Take Action Now. These resources are here to help you stop begging and start stewarding. Download the tools, join the communities, and visit the websites that equip you for financial dominion. Your economic transformation begins with action!

Testimonials from the Financial Rebellion 90-Day Coaching Program

Real experiences from participants who have experienced transformation through radical stewardship

"The most helpful [assignment] has been the vision and mission statements. It has allowed me to chart goals for where I see my finances in the future and create a vision and mission to work towards. I never thought of doing that when it came to my finances."
— W.D.

"The teachings... Hearing from others in a group setting, learning the breakdown of the scriptures, and truly hearing the Word of God. It has all been a valuable experience."
— P.N.

"Each teaching helps my mindset to shift, and each time I sit and do the homework, I notice my mindset shifts."
— C.P.

"The most valuable part is participating in this class with my wife. We are learning and changing our mindset together."
— D.W.

"I am not as fearful and stressed out over our finances as I have been before taking this class. I am understanding more and more to lean on God and Kingdom principles, not my own understanding."
— A.P.

"[There is] lots of encouragement and holding each other accountable."
— M.J.

"...it will cause you to wrestle with your thinking."
— R.J.

"[This] is helping me become a better person and having a closer connection to God. [I'm] on my way to becoming financially stable!"
— S.B.

"[The most valuable part is] The synergy of the group and Pastor Lexi's peaceful yet challenging demeanor and approach to how we work through each lesson. She has both caused us to be confronted with the truth and been holding us with white gloves throughout."
— J.R.

"[The journaling is] So impactful!... journaling allowed me to write down my past and current thoughts to evaluate alignment."
— J.C.

Join the Financial Rebellion 90-Day Coaching Program and take the next step toward financial freedom through Kingdom stewardship! Learn more at https://mm4h.life.

Are You Ready to Stop Begging and Start Stewarding?

For too long, believers have been begging God for financial breakthroughs while ignoring the principles of Kingdom stewardship. *Stop Begging God for Money* challenges everything you thought you knew about money, breaking the cycle of financial lack and replacing it with biblical wisdom, strategic action, and radical faith.

In this transformative guide, Dr. Lexi Johnson—an international speaker, licensed financial coach, and Kingdom entrepreneur—reveals the eight radical steps to taking control of your finances, aligning with Kingdom principles, and walking in financial dominion.

Inside, you'll discover how to:

✓ Transform your mindset and break free from financial bondage

✓ Heal from past financial mistakes and embrace true repentance

✓ Get organized, allocate wisely, and build financial stability

✓ Multiply your resources through the Four Storehouses principle

✓ Secure your legacy with estate planning and generational wealth transfer

No more waiting on a miracle. No more cycles of lack. It's time to steward your finances purposefully, build wealth the Kingdom way, and walk boldly in financial authority. It's time to produce, multiply, and dominate.

Are you ready?

Join the movement of Financial Rebels who have ditched begging and started stewarding!

Zephaniah Publishing

About the Author

Lexi Johnson is an international speaker, licensed financial coach, and strategist, Kingdom InPowered Network (KIN) co-founder, best-selling author, real estate investor, and graduate of The Goldman Sachs One Million Black Women—Black in Business Program (Cohort 6). She is also the Chief Stewardship Officer of Money Mastery 4 Her Enterprises and a pastor specializing in training missionaries and facilitating short-term international mission trips.

Between 2008 and 2011, God led Lexi through a series of devastating financial events that changed the landscape of her life. While such events may have crushed some, Lexi took the opportunity to draw closer to God, understand her purpose, and walk in it. Her speaking and teaching in finance, leadership, and purpose have led to widespread recognition for her transformational work in the U.S. and abroad.

Lexi holds a B.A. in Sociology, an M.B.A. in Business, an Honorary Doctorate, and a Global Fellowship in Christian Leadership. She also possesses multiple financial industry certifications and other recognized credentials. However, her greatest aspiration is to fulfill Genesis 1:28's mandate to produce, multiply, and dominate.

Connect with Lexi:

Email: lexi@mm4h.life

Website: mm4h.life

Facebook: @authordrlexij

Instagram, LinkedIn, TikTok: @thelexijohnson

www.ingramcontent.com/pod-product-compliance
Lightning Source LLC
Chambersburg PA
CBHW070207100426
42743CB00013B/3081